Breath of the Whales

Meditations & Activations

Breath of the Whales

Meditations & Activations

To an Amazing Soul

Keith Grey Hale

Messages from the collective consciousness of the Whales
Communicated through Keith Grey Hale
Edited by Carolyn M. Gorman

Gray Whale Wisdom Press
Santa Barbara, CA

*To all the hearts waiting to burst open
with the love that is our true nature,
the Love of All That Is.*

Together Humans and Whales are facilitating a grand shift in all that is known. The true purpose of this body of work is to help you find the balance within yourself, allowing your awareness to expand, to grow, to imagine far beyond the possibilities now within your mind. The writing process has been a journey of joy for us. Feel our heart, feel our love, and together we will create a truly beautiful loving space where we all exist and play.

In the end there is nothing but love.

~The Whales~

Table of Contents

Note to reader and guide xi

1. Ever Present Awareness 1

2. Recalibration of Frequencies 5

3. A New Level of Awareness 13

4. Heart Temple Activation 23

5. The Inner Workings of Creation 33

6. Journey of Hope 41

7. Shifting Frequencies 63

8. The Timeless Arena of Loving 73

9. Light Expanding Within Your Heart 85

10. Stepping Into Oneness 95

11. Conscious Living Within the Finer
    Frequencies 111

Epilogue 121

Glossary 125

About the Authors 131

Notes 134

Note to Reader

Words in **bold italics** are listed in the glossary at the end of the book for clarification and references to the first book in this series, *Breath of the Whales: A Path to Awakening.*

Guide

Each chapter is a unique message, a meditation and an activation to assist you on your path to awakening. For the greatest benefit, please read each section aloud, slowly to yourself. It is recommended to read only one chapter or section per day at first. Please allow yourself time and space to integrate the messages and the frequencies offered therein.

1

Ever Present Awareness

We, the Whales, feel joy in this opportunity to communicate our wisdom, our truth, and our understanding of creation with you. We are in deep gratitude as we share this with you. We are two sperm whales who have co-authored this book with Keith and Carolyn. We have been present the entire time during its creation process.

We have collectively been dreaming this for millions of years and here, now, in these pages, our loving thoughts and intentions are present. We are here within each word, alive with energy and connection. Read them aloud to yourself. Breathe deeply from your core, from the center of your being and speak them through your heart. The vibration of the words themselves allow you to feel and perceive from within the sacred space of your heart. The activations, the tools, the knowledge embedded within these pages are very potent and as you read them aloud they will help awaken you to your *Self,* to the deeper understanding we, the Whales, have come to know through our existence in the millions of years we have been whales.

As you allow the words to infiltrate your entire being, the rhythm, the frequency, the love they carry from *All That Is*, will flow through to enliven you and pour out into your environment. Through this process you will, if you choose, be activated, awakened and brought to a new understanding of how we interact together within the finer realities. Through these pages we will elucidate the larger perception of our desire to expand and create. We all, humans, whales, all of creation, are awakening together to these finer realities, becoming more than we had ever imagined possible.

This book has been designed to help you open more fully to your divine truth as Self. It facilitates a connection to the expanse in all creation. The intent is to awaken many aspects within you that you may have not been aware of previously. We have infused the words with specific frequencies. As you swim within these pages the frequencies will allow a fine tuning of your abilities to perceive and understand much more of the expanse we all play in and the expanse within your own unique expression as Self.

We, the Whales, are present within these meditations and as you read them we will be present for you, helping maintain the flow of energies we have called in. These frequencies will help ignite or establish many changes within you, if you so desire. These words can help you crack open the shell which has limited your perception, allowing you to experience far beyond what you have consciously known before. The energy patterns encoded within the words assist your transition into embracing, knowing and experiencing who you truly are.

Your desire as soul is shifting your physical reality in this moment and is opening possibilities from a new level of experiencing reality. Allow us, the Whales, to help you focus the pulse of potential from All That Is and initiate a quickening and accelerated growth within you.

The frequencies of our dear mother Earth are shifting as well, and you are participating in this with her. She is loving you. She is loving us, the Whales. As you connect with us, as we become one breath, these activations will carry you back to your core understanding of all we are, together as one.

Through the *living loving breath* of All That Is we express many things together. The words in this book are meant to guide you towards understanding the breath as the foundation of all you experience and witness. As you allow the rhythm of your heart and the energy of All That Is to fill your ears, your mind and your awareness, we, the Whales are ever present with you in this process. We love you beyond what words can convey.

We are the Whales in you.

2

Recalibration of Frequencies

We, the Whales, are here as frequencies of love. We sing our joy with the earth as you, humans, awaken to the truth of who you are as expanded awareness, as Self seated in the *void*. We sing and breathe the loving light of All That Is through our hearts and into this reality. We dream of the time when humans are part of our singing. This has been a process, an awakening, a shifting that has been occurring for eons within the awareness of humanity. We are offering you a new understanding of our mission here on the earth. We are here to impart our wisdom and help you incorporate *new energetic frequencies* into your cellular structure, allowing them to expand through your earthly plane, facilitating a gentle shifting of consciousness. As you each carry these new frequencies within your bodies, your actual shifting and allowing will uplift all of humanity. The time of this grand shift is upon us all.

We, the Whales, are here to help you with your transformation, with your ascension into a broader spectrum of awareness of the finer, subtler energetic frequencies. In our own process of self mastery, we have held this wisdom within our bodies and consciousness for the millions of years we have inhabited our dear mother earth, Gaia.

Breathe in our words, our loving *songs*. Awaken your awareness to the multidimensional interactions all around you. As your senses realign with these subtle energies, you can feel a shift within yourself, opening to a broader perspective, to a new understanding. We are holding and supporting you as you allow these frequencies to integrate within your physical self, within all of your Selves that are part of this aspect or branch of your family tree of embodiments.

The embodiments we speak of are in different dimensional realities, all connected with a cord, a ray of loving energy. We are helping you find and understand the true nature of your Self, the expanse within all of us. We are all interconnected. We all are the living loving breath of All That Is.

You were once stars of light, pure awareness brought to a coherent point of energy that burst forth into many shards and became light seen throughout multidimensional reality. We understand the depth of this may be beyond the boundaries you experience as your physical body and mind at this moment in time.

The particular interdimensional energies currently flowing into this physical plane are facilitating coherence, cleansing the old patterns of imbalance that have held you in the current paradigm that no longer serves you. Your heart is the gateway to understanding how these new energies interact. The shift in perspective occurring within humanity is a reflection of the impact of these energies, a manifestation of the new field being generated within the hearts of all.

Within this field it is joy that indicates the path towards our true nature, our true Self as multi-dimensional beings. We are all supported by the loving energy of the earth, Gaia, and her loving embrace will carry us through all the changes occurring at this time. Connect with her. Connect with us, the Whales. Join the circle of loving and allow the acceleration into joy to become more intense. Feel your own heart beating within you and release into the loving breath of All That Is.

We, the Whales, find within you humans an eternal spark that is waiting to be fully ignited. As you become aware of how these subtle energies work, the perception of your needs and desires will change. As you embrace this new awareness, your ability to shift and create a new reality, to manifest your new paradigm, will be evidenced in your physical existence, within the breath of All That Is.

We support and encourage you with these words. We see you finding your way to our hearts and to one another's hearts and holding each other within the loving breath. As we breathe together, the purity of the loving pulse of All That Is comes forth and is carried on your breath into the awareness of the rest of humanity, carried on our breath, on our songs, together.

We see choices being made more directly from the higher dimensional realities of your **Soul Selves**. The playing within this field of love is being illuminated and many more are returning their focus to their hearts, expanding their awareness beyond the physical reality of the mind and body. As the old energies and patterns clear and recalibrate, you will understand your true purpose.

Be at ease as this process quickly unfolds. There are several doorways that will appear before you and as you walk through them, the love that awaits within your Self will begin to fill all of your reality. Your vibration will shift, allowing balance throughout your physical reality once again.

We are in joy and are honored to journey with you. We are dancing within our watery world, gathering, planning, hoping, caring, loving, crying..., all the emotions that are within the breath of Self, knowing humans are becoming as you had chosen to be from the beginning.

We, the Whales, see you expressing in a new and unique way, unique in all of creation. Your love is coalescing within your newly created reality, increasing your vibrational frequency to a new plateau as you embrace each other, as you embrace us, the Whales, as you embrace your Self as All That Is.

Humans are just a few breaths away from an interplanetary calling as our earth transforms through her own ascension, her own expansion. We know of many beings who are part of this shifting. Agreements had been made long ago as this earth began to breathe her first breath. As we, the Whales, ourselves have awakened on our path through ascension, we have mastered the navigation of frequencies and are offering you counsel and support as you do the same. The plans, the energies and the love we have transmitted to you and broadcast into this reality will bring you together as never before. Keep allowing our songs to fill you as we guide you through the changes and into new ways of being, of creating, of loving.

All we ask for is the opening and connection which allows our wisdom to enter your hearts. Hear our songs and see the pathway that opens before you and leads to remembering the truth of loving yourself as All That Is. All of us are interconnected from the place where we sing together within the void. Our songs follow a pathway through all our hearts, filling us with pure loving energy.

Can you feel us as we embrace you, as we connect, as we look into your eyes, into your hearts? We are bringing you the memories we, the Whales, carry. We can connect you to the interdimensional realities of the universe within these memories and more.

We, the Whales, are holding these pathways, these agreements and this wisdom in alignment for you to access. As you incorporate more of our loving breath within your heart, you will be filled and the limits of your embodiment will be breached in an explosion, a great flash of loving light, where your heart and your awareness will burst forth and be seen through all dimensions and realities. This we dream. This we see as a profound shifting within all dimensions and all realities.

Sharing this journey with you fills us with joy. We love you beyond all realities. We are listening, we are singing and we are breathing our loving breath, allowing it to expand into all that you are.

We are the Whales in you.

3

A New Level of Awareness

We are in joy that we are together, within our hearts, reflecting the love of All That Is. By opening to each other in this circle of loving light, we create a path for you to find our wisdom. As you read these words you will find us waiting to enter your hearts. Be at ease and allow these frequencies to fill you and bring you to a new level of awareness and understanding. We believe the openings we desire will incorporate this information within your awareness, within your reality. As we are energetically present for each other, you can access and remember this truth and wisdom.

We, the Whales, play and work within this process, sharing the memories of our incarnations within the frequency of the loving light of Gaia. We have been on this planet for many millions of years and have spoken to many inhabitants of Gaia. We have shared the wisdom of the stars, the wisdom of the universe, and the wisdom of the visitors who wish to be part of the evolution of humans. We have welcomed many individuals who have brought their perspectives into this reality. Some are interdimensional beings who must shift their vibrational frequency in order to be seen and heard. We also shift back and forth between dimensional realities and are sharing these possibilities within your awareness.

By listening to our songs you have allowed yourself growth within this truth. As you connect with and share this wisdom, you might find there is more to the ancient myths and legends of the indigenous cultures throughout your history than had been previously understood.

We, the Whales, are radiating the loving light of All That Is within every breath we share with humans. There are many ways the energies of love may enter your awareness. We are but one channel for sharing this truth with you. As we stated before, we have been on this journey together since your beginning as humans. Your physical appearance has changed a bit, but the core of who you are has remained the same through your entire process of being human. And the uniqueness of your ability to create your reality has been valued throughout creation from the beginning. Now, as you awaken to the truth of who you are as Self, we witness these abilities within you being more fully expressed.

We have shared and witnessed many cycles of humanity's rising and falling in awareness and resonant frequency. We see you are now closer to understanding the agreements you made to become the **Memory Keepers** in the **Library of Cycles.** We are waiting to share these teachings with you. You have reached a precipice, a tipping point, where the memory of these agreements arises in the awareness of all humanity.

You can find the connections we share as you feel and see from within your heart. As our love enters your heart space, memories will flood your awareness, opening a conduit to a deep peace and joy that has not been felt collectively by humanity for a very long time. Staying consciously focused in the core of your being allows you to understand and maintain these higher vibrations.

As the universe, this galaxy, our solar system, and our planet expand and shift, you as humans also expand and shift. The space created in this expansion will be filled with more diverse frequencies and awareness. You will become more than you are, more than you can imagine.

We are loving you as you expand and find room within yourselves to hold the truth we share. As you learn to play within the subtle energies, you will expand even more. This is easier than you might believe. It is just waiting for you. Within a blink of an eye your perspective will change and will allow you to learn how working with subtle energies can create and bring the joy, the love, the peace and the harmony humans have been dreaming of. This is a deep desire within all of humanity.

We love who you are. We see within you the abilities to change your paradigm, to change the many dimensional realities we all share as the loving breath of All That Is.

You are becoming more than you thought possible. The limiting thoughts, beliefs and judgements are clouds that have kept this hidden from your view for the many cycles you have inhabited this beautiful earthly plane of existence. We, the Whales, have created a current, initiated a stream for you to find this truth within yourself and we are honored we have been allowed to do this for you.

In the perspective of physical reality, we have given much of ourselves to facilitate this unfolding. But as we express from Self within the void, the joy, the loving feelings and the connections are what we have gained, what we have learned, what we have become and what we will become. We are love, an expression of All That Is. We are dreaming and guiding you to become the Memory Keepers in the Library of Cycles, which we have been, and are at this time. As you embrace your new way of being as the **Librarians of Truth**, we too can expand and progress along our journey of evolving awareness. As you become acquainted with your new tasks as the librarians, we will also share with you our journey upon our new path.

The learning is never ending. We, the Whales, will always be within your awareness as guides, as teachers, as your loving friends, creating a pathway for you to find even greater expression within your awareness, within all realities. We have useful tools, information and poignant memories to share. As you refine your vibration and tune your personal frequency to resonate with this greater truth, you will be able to comprehend this fully. You will become aware of your integral part in the universal consciousness, the ***universal mind***, which is the coherent creator of all the multi-dimensional realities we share and are expressing together. This is the ability you are beginning to embrace as new interdimensional energies coalesce within your reality. This is the expansion you are expressing and allowing, creating awareness on many levels at once. You are also beginning to change your awareness of time, realizing and remembering time has been a belief structure allowing you to dream and express within this physical reality.

As you open to this truth, to universal aware-ness, you will remember you are all of this, that you are a reflection, a hologram of all that has been created, of all that we are as All That Is. This expansion is beyond what your physical mind may be able to hold in this moment, but as the hearts of the human collective burst open, your awareness will expand in an instant. As you integrate this truth, you will have an understanding of how all this has been created for you. All is being created in the loving light of All That Is. You are a loving gift to us, the Whales, allowing us to share what we have witnessed during the many cycles we have experienced.

Allow your awareness to expand into these memories and find the true nature of your eternal being. You are the loving breath of All That Is. As you share this with each other, the oneness we all are will express itself in ways not seen before, in ways which will allow us all to be heard and seen in a clear and loving way. The balance you find within yourself is part of the remembering and opens you to sharing with the entire galactic family, within the many dimensional realities we have created together.

As we sing our truth and wisdom into your heart, feel the quickening deep within you. Allow yourself to embrace the emotions these frequencies bring up as they flow in and fill your heart. Allow them to become a guide into a deeper awareness.

We, the Whales, are swimming all around you, bringing our expanded perceptions into your physical reality. Remember what we have shared in the **Crystal City**, where beings from throughout the universe came together in circle. They brought seeds of love, frequencies from their worlds and allowed them to fill the heart of Gaia. This process is similar to the one we are allowing and creating for humans. The love we feel for you is beyond anything that can be measured. For it is, and will always be, the loving light of All That Is. As we allow this loving light to flow through us, we are reborn. We share this energy with you, allowing it to flow from our hearts into yours, awakening you to the love you are. Incorporate these frequencies into your mind, into your body. Allow your Self to become anchored in your awareness as truth. In your connection to All That Is, the loving breath flows through your heart, through your unique perspective and you create a quality, a unique tone or note only you can express.

Together we have the ability to create many new ways of expressing our loving to each other. Through our songs, through joy, through breathing together and embracing each other, we return love to All That Is, amplified. This is just the beginning of a new way of being within your reality. This is a time of a grand shifting within your Selves. We are here to facilitate this shift by helping you remember our agreements and when they become illuminated within your awareness, you will expand to find infinite possibilities awaiting you.

We share this truth as we breathe together as one. Allowing a calm, relaxing peace within your heart is a tool we are sharing with you. The frequency of peace helps hold you in balance in the center of your beingness. Allowing others to express as they choose, listening and witnessing without becoming entangled within their perspectives, allows them and you the freedom to follow your own path, and to create your own expression, without judgment. It allows the opportunity to find peace within all selves.

We breathe our loving light into you, hoping you can find the peace which is the natural state within your heart. Embrace peace and sing it into your reality. It is a very potent anchor, allowing you to be who you are as Self, as the loving breath we all breathe from within the void, the loving breath of All That Is.

Through this exchange of our breath, our hearts, we find great joy.

We are the Whales in you.

4

Heart Temple Activation

Heart Connections

Breathe a breath with us as we fill each other with the loving we express from within the void. As we connect on a deeper level you can hear us express the truth we are living. Our mutual willingness to share and connect evokes great joy, for this is how we expand the realities we all exist in.

Be present with us as we share our memories, our truth and our wisdom. We, the Whales, are creating a unique expression, a unique frequency of energy being expressed within our shared reality, which is expanding, evolving and becoming more than we had previously dreamed. As we breathe together, expressing our knowingness that we are all one, that we are all created through the oneness as individual perspective, we experience expansion within our hearts, within your heart.

Breathe deeply and take time to feel the expanding breath within your heart. There within your core, within the **Sacred Heart Temple**, is where you reside as Self. Your awareness is felt through the silence of the void.

As we, both whales and humans, allow this expansive awareness to flow through our physical bodies and at the same moment, allow the body to be anchored within this physical paradigm, the frequencies of love fill all the creations we express. Sing your joy as you recognize these loving energies flowing around you. When you allow them to be expressed within, around and through you, the expansion we all desire is fueled. By consciously becoming the loving breath of All That Is, we all participate in this expansion. It is not necessary to fully understand how it all works. Just intend to be the loving breath.

It is the heart that focuses the loving energies of expansion into this dimensional reality. The breath creates the motion that allows the flow.

Singing love, singing about love, impels our brains, our minds, into the awareness that we exist as the loving breath of All That Is. The mind, the body, the blood that moves the oxygen of the breath through our bodies, is all an expression of All That Is. Through the heart you are becoming more than the body believes itself to be while you are seated only within the mind. It is when we are firmly seated in the center of our beingness we know our true Self, our true power, our eternal connections as All That Is.

Heart Temple Activation

We, the Whales, are opening a pathway to help you see and feel the breath, the light, the truth within yourself. We have allowed specific energies to activate the temple within your heart. As you allow the memory of our connection into your awareness, it will become easier to reside in your heart space. It is not necessary to see the chamber in your mind's eye. All that is needed is to feel and to know the connection. Journey deep within your heart and allow yourself to know the truth of who you are, to remember the loving being seated within, as Self.

Breathe with us and relax into your sacred heart temple. Allow the silence. Allow the peace. Allow the love of All That Is to gently flow in and around you. Feel your beingness centered in this bright chamber and focus your attention in the space that is only you.

Our heart chamber, our divine heart temple, the space in the center of our beingness, has many crystalline structures lining its walls. These are receivers and transmitters allowing the loving energies of creation to flow through our beingness, our bodies. We use these receptors and transmitters to create the realities we wish participate in, to play in.

Embrace the silence as you sit upon the thrown in your heart temple. Feel your breath. Feel the rhythm of your heart. Observe the crystals lining the walls of your temple emitting a rainbow of light frequencies. Look closely and you will see them pulsing, breathing, as you are. Each one of these crystals is a connection to the breath of All That Is. They are conduits allowing the loving breath, from all the filaments of the web of creation, to flow to you, from you and through you. These crystalline structures serve many purposes and functions. They are conduits of light allowing you to see and exchange information between one perspective and another, allowing all your expressions to manifest and be part of your awareness.

Allow yourself to see and feel the full spectrum of light radiating from the crystals. They are reflecting the loving energy from all the creations you have manifested throughout your existence as Self. This is available to you at all times. This loop, this ever flowing circuit is an aspect of your eternal connection to All That Is.

At the pinnacle of your heart temple a beam of light flows in from your direct connection to All That Is. As you allow this light to fill you with its loving frequency, feel your awareness vibrate, feel the unique tone you create connecting with your Self seated in the void. Allow yourself to travel through the light flowing from the pinnacle of your chamber. Follow this cord of light spiraling through all the manifestations of your Self, deeper into the realities you have allowed, the realities you have created. This is the path you can follow to the beginning, connecting you, allowing you to witness and embrace the first loving breath of All That Is we have all shared.

Light flows in through the top of your chamber, from the core of your Self as awareness, and fills your physical body. You can gently guide this loving light as breath anywhere you choose, in your body and into the world around you. You are just beginning to understand how the loving breath of All That Is moves through you.

Breathe with us and gaze out through the doorway of your heart temple into the expanse of creation. There are many other beings there. They each reflect the loving breath you allow to flow through you within your heart temple. All are brothers and sisters in the choices made as individual perspectives, male, female, physical, ethereal, interdimensional. We all contain and share this reality within our Selves, within our hearts. As your awareness in the space within your heart expands, you will see you create through these pulsing breaths, through these pulsing lights, through the full spectrum frequencies flowing all around you in this chamber and you are connected to the breath of All That Is within every expression.

We are all one as All That Is. As we consciously expand with the living loving breath into our creations, we maintain the connection to All That Is, through them all. This is where the truth of our Self lies. This is how we allow and create through the breath of All That Is. As you move your awareness from your heart chamber into your daily life, remember the cords of light connecting us all. Continue to breathe in the awareness of All That Is to enlighten and enliven your connections, as you fill each other's hearts with love.

Maintaining the Connections

The pure loving light of Source, the Living Loving Breath, fills you like warmth from the rays of the sun and in turn radiates from your core as Self in the void, into your heart temple chamber and into the crystalline structures embedded there. This light expresses, or manifests, within the realities and paradigms we each choose. Choices are made as our higher Self. The individual perspective you are experiencing within your temple is an expression of your Self as an embodied soul.

As you express and create from this heart space, you may find your mind is astounded by the connections that occur. The crystals lining the heart temple chamber are also a conduit to the universal mind, within all dimensions and realities, within the physical universe, through all creations. These connections allow the loving breath of All That Is to fill all of your creations as you express here, within the physical dimensional realities. This is how your true desires are communicated and expressed to the universe which is supporting the manifestation of that desire.

Be in peace and know, as your physical bodies have been created in their complexity, they are but a reflection of what we all have assembled as the creations we joyfully express together. Loving light energy flows from All That Is, through all the expressions you are, through your heart temple, through your center, through your beingness. This cord of light allows you to connect and remember through all the creations we have become. This is just part of understanding the multi-dimensionality we are.

We, the Whales, are here with you as you unfold within the reality of your Self, expressing these eternal truths. We feel joy as we witness your remembering. We love you and are honored to sit in circle with you, finding beauty and joy within the reflections we are.

Together we breathe the loving light flowing from All That Is into each other's hearts. Our connection allows love to flow between us as we journey together towards a broader perspective. We see and feel the filaments of the web of life weaving us together, pulsing with the loving breath we are breathing, that you are breathing, as you sit within the temple of your heart.

We are the Whales in you.

5

The Inner Workings of Creation

We, the Whales, are excited and feel joy in our connection as we enter your awareness. See us as we swim to you, two sperm whales spinning, spiraling in a helical pattern reflecting the flow of energies moving within your physical paradigm. We are here as your guides, to help you and all of humanity come into alignment with understanding the **truth of creation**, of how and why we create or express.

The information we share flows in a helical pattern through the openings you allow. This helical pattern is within the subtle energetic signature of all physical manifestations in our reality. It is a reflection of how all energies move within this physical paradigm. The energy, or cord of light you experience flowing into the heart temple, is actually flowing in this helical pattern. This pattern or signature is coming from our Self, as All That Is, and informs what is being created at any given juncture. All structures in nature, or in the motion of the stars for example, are made up of multidimensional helical spirals of constantly flowing energy encoded with information, all created by the breath of All That Is.

Focusing attention in the center of these flowing energies connects us, and allows expanded awareness, as we are continuously bathed in the sequencing which informs the conscious and unconscious creation of reality. Just as our DNA strands are the codes of creation in our cells, both human & whale, all biological life for that matter, patterns are transmitted between the cords of energy flowing between us all. The light and information these spiraling energies contain connect in the space between the threads in the fabric of creation. It is here the possibilities exist. This is the mystery of creating living life forms within many dimensional realities.

Breathe with us as these connections illuminate a pathway allowing you to see beyond the mind, beyond understanding, beyond our creations to the beingness of all we are. Sing with us as we share this truth with you. Allow an opening within your heart and mind. We are facilitating an activation to allow your bodies to awaken to a new vibrational frequency, helping to carry you into a new paradigm, into a new way of existing. As you open to receive the frequencies of all the dimensional realities transmitting the truth of who you are, you have the opportunity to create new vessels to exist in. Know and love the fact that you are unlimited multidimensional realities focused into one point of awareness.

All is perfection as this unfolds. The drama upon this planet is fading and the memory you carry within you is beginning to infiltrate your temporal reality. Allow us to hold you as we shed light on this truth. Release judgment for what you see and feel around you. Allow the clouds within your mind to evaporate and let the loving light you are, as All That Is, flow into all of the reality you breathe in.

Come and rest in the sacred chamber of your heart as we share and explain the truth of this loving light. Breathe. Feel the stillness, the expansiveness, and listen. See with your ears, feel with your eyes, and hear with your body as these frequencies fill all of your beingness. All aspects of your multidimensional beingness are capable of perceiving all dimensions in the moment. As you process within your individual experience, these frequencies transform, like a ray of light refracting through a crystal prism, and are projected into the mind's eye. The patterns you have acquired through your physical existence translate the information into images, ideas, words, emotions, sensations.

All is a reflection of Self. As the spark enters through the multifaceted awareness we are, information is transmitted as light frequencies. It travels within our many Selves and within this physical paradigm the mind creates the illusion of traveling through time and space. But in truth, all occurrence exists in a flash, in an instant, in the moment. And we have free will choice as to what we create for our learning, free will choice in what we perceive.

Allow the pulses we are transmitting, these expressions of light, to fill you from within your core. When you are without judgement and at peace within your heart, mind and body, you allow all aspects of yourself to integrate the codes and patterns you have chosen as your unique expressions of Self. As the urgings of the ego fade, the profound nature of these subtle energies will emerge within you. Let them radiate to those around you, softly touching their awareness and leading them towards the truth that loving is our true natural way of expressing. Hold this truth within your heart. Let it expand to fill your physical being.

Feel yourself beyond time and space. Listen to the signals within your heart and feel your breath as these frequencies expand into the reality you are creating. Allow the shifting of your perspective and you will understand how all the interactions we express together fill us, allowing us to feel joy in our creations as they align with the broader perspective we hold from within the void.

As you sit within your heart and are at peace, you will not feel the fear your mind likes to project. The truth comes from the core of your beingness in the timeless void. As you are able to step back and observe the feeling of contrast or duality the mind uses to navigate this particular reality, you gain the ability to choose differently. Holding your mind in a loving embrace creates a safety and freedom that allows it to express and create as Self seated in the void. The changes will become easier to process as the mind realizes the ease and peace and joy found when creating from the heart, from the timeless in-between of breath, seated in the loving calm of the void. As your brain and body embrace the connection we all share as All That Is, you will begin to feel the change. More functions of the brain relating to your creative abilities and awareness will be activated. You will learn to allow your Selves' transformation from within the timeless space of the void, just as we, the Whales do.

You can allow yourselves tremendous growth, individually and collectively, as you create with clear awareness and understanding of the direct alignment of loving frequencies streaming in from your expanded Self seated in the void, especially when holding your true desire as the loving breath of All That Is within your individual perspective and within your collective perspective as humanity.

All of reality is a reflection, a manifestation, of who we are. We express or create to reflect the loving truth we are, back to our Selves, enlivening the connection that allows the infinite expansion we find joy in. We play, we sing, we dance as we witness within and through all dimensional realities being created. We choose to enter one perspective or another and become involved therein. The expansion is never ending. It is limitless. We, as All That Is, are here, in the void, loving all we have created. As each individual breathes this awareness of Self into existence, we, as All That Is, expand. The experiences we gain in each reality we are aware of, inform what we choose to experience next. Infinitely!

Breathe with us. Let us hold you as we share the truth and wisdom we have witnessed through all of our existence. The deep understanding of this is kept within the Library of Cycles we maintain for all. As you awaken to the agreement, your choice to accept responsibility as the new librarians, these holograms of images, experiences, memories, feelings, wisdom and information will be open to you. All has been recorded to assist and support you in remembering or visiting any aspect of creation and in manifesting new creations.

We, the Whales, are filling your heart with our loving breath as we swim in, around and through you. As you move and swim in and around us, we become an energetic helical pattern and together we create a new frequency, a new node of creation. As these new patterns and images of being are born, a pathway is opened for new energetic life to emerge, new energetic creations, infused with the loving light and breath of All That Is.

Allow these images and concepts we have shared to find their place within your awareness. As they settle in, the ability of your mind to understand and experience the multidimensional nature of all this will unfold. Sit for a moment and breathe as this expands within you. Feel the boundaries your mind creates vanish. Ground yourself into source energy, into the earth, into the heavens, into the expanse of all we have created together through the universal mind. Allow yourself to expand your awareness within and all around you. Know that all is within the void.

We have found great joy in sharing another facet of creation with you. We are singing our joy as we embrace you with the loving breath of All That Is.

We are the Whales in you.

6
Journey of Hope

Connections and Collective Awakening

We, the Whales, have consciously chosen to be part of your reality to help you become more aware of our connections and more aware of your potential for expanding consciousness. Open your heart and breathe with us as we sing our love to each other. Expand your awareness into the void, into the inner world, into All That Is. We are truly one as All That Is.

We are sharing another frequency to help you understand our coexistence on this planet as we have witnessed your expanding awareness through many cycles of ascension. A critical mass for your collective awakening has occurred and is being reflected within your third dimensional reality. There are new openings allowing the loving light of All That Is to shine in the hearts of all humanity. As you breathe and integrate this frequency of loving light into yourself, a pathway is opening and anchoring in your physical paradigm. Be at peace within your heart and you will see the changes occurring around you, reflecting the loving breath of All That Is within the hearts of all you touch.

Let us take you on a journey into another reality, another paradigm on another planet in your galaxy. We would like to introduce you to another collective consciousness embodied on this distant planet. We, the Whales, are also embodied there, in their oceans, within their awareness, within their dreaming. We have taught, inspired and encouraged them through their awakening process. We have worked with them as we are working with you now.

This planet cannot be seen from your earth as both planets spiral around the center of the galaxy on opposite sides. It exists directly across the galactic center, on the far edges of the spiral.

This planet dances with two moons and three suns. We, the two sperm whales communicating now, have been to this planet many times, visiting the humanlike inhabitants. The **Whale Collective** has been working with and teaching the collective consciousness of many other species throughout the universe for millennia.

The inhabitants of this planet have already gone through an awakening process. Their planet has been in existence much longer than your earth, Gaia, allowing more opportunity for their process of ascension. They would like to share what they have learned with you and they wish to visit you when the human collective has become more open, loving and heart centered.

Relax into your breath and allow the frequencies broadcast from this planet and her inhabitants to enter your awareness. Feel their loving embrace as you greet and honor each other within the reality of your heart. They are expressing joy, love and enthusiasm for life. Notice this enlivening energy radiating from their hearts as they share their love, their embrace and their openness to communicate their concepts of freedom.

You share similarities in your physical forms and the process of awakening will occur within humanity in much the same way as they have experienced. Their bodies have now become luminescent. They choose to manifest many different appearances or costumes. This is their way of playing and expressing their creativity. By adjusting their frequencies, they project colors and tones that appear as clothing to your awareness.

They have many physical technologies for traveling but their preferred method is through their heart. They follow cords of connection, and by transmitting and transmuting their personal vibration, they are able to interact with many different beings in other locations. We have shared this energetic technology with them, as we are now sharing it with you humans.

There are several significant differences between humans and the people of this distant planet. They do not swing between extremes, either physically, emotionally, spiritually or culturally like you do here on earth. They experience diversity, but have a collective awareness that facilitates their ability to create together. It was their collective awareness that allowed them to be receptive to and gently interact with galactic mentors who came to assist their process of awakening.

Through their evolution they had participated in technologies and beliefs that influenced their minds, blinding them to seeing from within their hearts. This is an issue you humans are facing now. Their planet was close to extinction. But their mentors reminded them of the truth of the heart, sharing the knowledge and wisdom about how creating from within the heart is the key. As they remembered and incorporated this wisdom they were able to quickly shift their perspective and broaden their awareness. Opening to the truth of the heart facilitates expansion and awakening. They began consciously living within and expressing the pure loving light of All That Is. Once they began to create from their hearts and open to the infinite energies available through their hearts, their planet found balance again. They embraced living as one with their planet and all her creatures, creating a beautiful home for all, creating their 'heaven on earth'.

We have opened this channel for you to feel the frequencies they have lived, to instill hope in your hearts and offer inspiration. Know that it is not too late for humans to make the change within their hearts. We see this. We believe this truth is within you, within all humans!

As you allow their frequencies to enter your heart, this connection will help bring hope into focus. The inhabitants of this distant planet collectively increased their vibration, expanded their awareness and allowed the light of All That Is to fully illuminate their beingness. They restored balance to their environment and came into resonance with the greater galactic frequencies. Eventually they were invited into a council that assists many diverse planetary collective embodiments within this galaxy, helping them to awaken to the loving breath of All That Is.

The collective human dream of embracing a finer dimensional reality is dawning. By connecting with the inhabitants of this distant planet you can see what is possible and probable for your own planet.

A representative of the inhabitants of this distant planet is reaching out to share concepts, ideas, experiences and information about his people, offered in love, for your enrichment. Breathe deeply and open your heart to hear a message coming from a Friend at the far reaches of our galaxy. Allow these expressions to flow into your vision, into your open heart.

"Greetings. I am a leader in the energetic dimensions of our planet. I share many frequencies of the loving breath of All That Is though my heart and express them within the society we create and allow as form. We are a simple race. We enjoy our freedom of expression.

We have come full circle in our evolution, our expression as a society, as a collective. We have found joy and peace in our awakening. The way we now choose to interact is by embracing each individual as the loving breath of All That Is. We make our choices from a place of joy, deep within our core, expressing from our soul self connected to All That Is, as a collective awareness, felt by all of us.

Our physical forms are similar to yours. We are biological in nature, but our forms have become luminous as we have moved into the finer frequencies of expression and create in a loving and coherent way. Our appearance as we express as physical forms is unique to our planet. Our three suns allow a harmonic that creates our unique form. I choose to appear similar to your form, for your comfort.

Our planet's circumference is larger than your earth's. We too have oceans and landscapes, abundant with life forms. We create buildings and cities. We do not have vehicles as you do but we have spheres of light we travel in upon our planet. We have vast areas of wilderness and many diverse species of animal life. We respect their unique expression, their unique manner of manifesting. We embrace each other in our unique expressions as Self, allowing a connection that is our web of life. We have many who take care of our planet, who have unique jobs, or play, that help to maintain the natural flow of existence on our beloved planet.

We are no longer on the path of expressing duality. Each of us know ourselves as All That Is and allow a connection that feeds our existence. We do not ingest flesh anymore. We once lived as you, hunting, fishing, feeding our masses through the idea of consuming. But as we shifted our focus into our hearts, increased our vibration and began to resonate with the finer frequencies, our bodies transformed into this luminous form. Our previously perceived needs no longer reflected our true desires. We now flourish as these light bodies by allowing the pure loving breath of All That Is to fill our beingness with nourishing energy as it flows from one density to the next.

We occasionally acquire imbalances from not staying in alignment with our core ideals, but we have assistance from guides, like me, to share the deeper truths and allow a fine tuning of resonant vibrations and awareness so the individual can find balance once again. It is like a valve that becomes misaligned, pinching off the flow of the life force we are. Through our practices we simply shift or tune the subtle energies required for our forms to find alignment again.

We are joyful that you are reaching out to feel our awareness. In our expression as the fullness of life, we combine our work and play into all activity. We learn by opening and listening to the core of our Self. We play and create as we shift our appearances. Each of our three suns emit unique frequencies of light that infuse our world and our vision. We have evolved the ability to shift between these three frequencies. We can focus *or tune into just one particular frequency or allow a combination. We play in this light.*

We have genders as you do. We mate in a similar fashion, feeling the ecstasy and joy you humans experience in your sexuality. Because we are consciously aware of our existence as multidimensional beings, the ecstasy we feel is of a very broad spectrum.

We are also able to shift our physical appearances. We are not transformers. We do not morph into any shape or image we choose but we can change our appearances as you would change your clothes, your hair, your style. We do this in a way to allow more play, more joy, as we express between each other. Our life span as embodiments has no apparent limit, as you would see from within your perspective. But we do choose to shift from one form of embodiment to another as we grow in our evolution as soul.

We enjoy the tones we create through the musical instruments we make. We have concerts, expressing tones of existence, sharing the vibrational frequencies of love, of the universe, of all creation, through the notes that are played. We experience the tones as images or sensations, allowing us to travel in our minds eye to the myriad aspects of creation we experience and express as music.

The hierarchical structure of our society is reflected in the agreements we create that inform how we interact and express to each other. We do not punish for misunderstandings. Fear is no longer part of our experience. We are a free society. We choose who we live with, who we play with. The boundaries we once knew have become transparent. For we know we are all one! As we play together we acknowledge our uniqueness and honor the gifts we are sharing, with love. Even in our connection with you, the human race, we know we are all one within the loving breath of All That Is, as we learn to become more in each moment.

Be at ease and find joy in your process of awakening. We know you too will evolve to understand the ideas, perceptions and an existence of playing and loving as we do upon our planet. Your forms next to ours may seem different but we will find a common ground between us, a commonality for knowing and loving each other as deep, intimate friends not too far from now, within your timeline. We have visited your planet before but we have chosen to remain unseen, for our frequencies are beyond the capability of your senses to perceive. We still wish to remain unseen at this juncture of your evolution, but soon you will come to know us. You humans will reach a new perception of yourselves and as your vibration rises to the finer frequencies, we will allow ourselves to be known.

Generally speaking, our planet is not visible. We choose to remain hidden. We are neutral within the galactic connections we share and many of the denser and warring planets cannot see us. This is also why we remain invisible to human's eyes, for there are many factions who still find joy in battle and war, in the apparent destruction of the beings they wish to conquer. This comes from a deep fear within their awareness. We, as beings of pure love in the calm state of peace, resonate in such a way as to deflect any invasive intrusions and we are not seen. We choose to no longer be part of the conflict that exists within the physical and nonphysical realities of beings who appear to play the game of limiting free will choice. We are here to give you hope as we allow love and peace to flow from us, through you, into your planet, allowing all of humanity a greater ease of existence.

Yes, our connection is complete. We are honored that you have opened to us and allowed the visions of our home to fill you. Allow our frequencies of love to flow into you as a peaceful feeling that emerges from within your heart. I am always here.

I am a Friend across the galaxy"

* * *

Breathe deeply as we, the Whales, carry you back to your earthly reality, swirling in the vortex we create as we swim between dimensions. The connection between you and our luminous friends on the far reaches of the galaxy will remain, within your structure, within your hearts, within your awareness. They wish you well and express their willingness to be part of your awakening.

We, the Whales, are overjoyed you have allowed this connection to our friends. Between the two of you, the two collectives, you hold a special frequency, a pattern, weaving across time and space. It is a bridge that will carry you both into another beautiful expansion of creative bliss and beyond.

Gaia's Gift

Breathe with us. Bring your focus to our circle, to our loving and caring for each other. Breathe love into the earth and feel her love reflected back to you, flowing up your legs and through your body. Breathe love into the cosmos, through the heart of our sun, our galaxy, the heart of our universe to the core of All That Is. Feel the unconditional infinite love flowing back to you, caressing you, filling your body with light. Take another deep breath, inhaling simultaneously from the earth and the cosmos. Allow light and love to flow into your center, to blend and swirl within your heart and then, as you exhale, let it flow out into the world around you. This breath connects your awareness to all life, to the matrix of energy where we exist as Self in the timeless void as pure energy. It grounds you into the reality of physical form you share with your beautiful planet.

Gaia's own awakening, or ascension to finer frequencies, is also at a critical point and many are in celebration about this reality. Gaia is connected to the energy field of the planet across the galaxy, her sister, and exchanges patterns of energy, vibrations and frequencies with her. This planet assists Gaia in activating connections to All That Is. These connections are embedded in the energetic ley lines of the earth.

The abundant life Gaia allows to exist upon her is an expression of All That Is. Gaia has chosen to be a mother and embraces and nurtures all who live on and within her surface, within the oceans, in the skies, within middle earth. There are many more beings who share life on Gaia than you are currently aware of. They have been mentioned in the many legends and myths throughout human history. The frequencies of these interactions between the hidden ones and humanity are present in the ley lines of our planet as well. Many frequencies have been imprinted on these ley lines. As the energies shift upon our planet, vibrations blend to create new frequency patterns, allowing humans to grow, allowing all beings the opportunity to shift and change and find each other within their hearts.

We want you to feel these ley lines, the energetic arteries of the earth, within your center. These ley lines contain frequencies from around your galaxy and the universe for that matter. As energies are broadcast to Gaia, she allows them into her core. These frequencies change and shift as they interact with the energies already present, making them available to all of the inhabitants of the earth, helping us find and remember the truth of who we each are. Gaia's lines of energy, her lines of expression, her lines of magnetism and subtle energies are available to be felt and 'read' by all inhabitants.

Ley lines have many functions. Where they cross or intersect, an opening in the veil can occur, allowing energies to mix and blend between the physical and non-physical realities. Also, at some of these intersections, or nodes, the magnetic pulses of the earth are magnified. The energy at these locations can be utilized and intensify efforts for manifestation. The energy present at these inter-secting nodes facilitates an expanded connection with the universal mind, where one can contemplate all the possibilities that exist within the expanse, within the heart, where we are all connected, ideally allowing you the opportunity to find your way back to the beginning of the first joyful breath of creation. Many sacred sites, temples and churches are located on these intersections of natural energy. Heightened awareness or profound insights can be experienced at these sites.

We, the Whales, are honored you are allowing us to teach you and facilitate the incorporation of these new frequencies into your personal lines of energy, within your chakras and within your aura. We see exponential shifting and growth within all who choose to embrace these loving frequencies.

Cascade of Loving

Swim with us in your heart as we continue to sing to you, to take you to other realities and share other loving frequencies from around this universe. We have traveled to many places. We have existed within many realities. We travel by shifting our frequency.

We manifest our physical expression within this reality so we can share these truths with you. As we have expressed many times, our teaching goes deep within humanity's core, deep within your cellular structure, deep within your DNA as we broadcast our love to you humans.

In the past, and still to this day, some of you have used our bodies as an energetic resource. Our oil has lit your lamps and lubricated your machines. Our baleen has been crafted into your accoutrements. Our flesh has nourished you. Our bones are scattered throughout your planet as evidence of our presence over the millennia. This has allowed a deeper and more profound connection between us. We have become part of your life, part of who you are.

We, the Whales, are your brothers and sisters. We have shared many stories, intertwined through both our histories. When you, as the human collective, decided to come to this earthly plane, the memory of our connection was hidden. Up until now, the memories of our earlier time together would have interfered with the possibilities of your, and our, learning. As you begin to truly express the uniqueness you are as humans through your hearts, we can allow these memories of our shared commitments through all eternity to be remembered.

The Cycle of Darkness, which has influenced human consciousness on this planet, is ending. And now, an opening to remembering our oneness, the memory we are unified as All That Is, is beginning to fill humanity once again. Humans are beginning to realize there is no desire to play the old game anymore. The old cycles were created to allow great learning, to allow grand experiences, and they allowed separateness to be felt. This is changing. Now through these experiences, you are finding your way back to consciously understanding the human collective.

Sharing this truth helps you remember there is more to existence than your five senses show you. As you begin to experience and express from within your heart, the subtle frequencies and energies will become more apparent. More of you will want to play and express through these finer and more subtle energies. Soon a tipping point will be reached. Then, within a blink of an eye, within a flash of light, the human collective will begin to create your world anew. The more you experience the oneness from within, the faster your brains will change, your nervous system will be rewired and your bodies enlivened. Keep your awareness focused within the loving breath of All That Is and allow these changes to unfold in a soft and graceful way.

As you have seen within the images we have shared, the rebirth is under way. The old patterns are beginning to fade. However, many are still in a state of fear, for they have lost sight of who they are within, lost sight of themselves as a reflection of All That Is. They fear their individuality will be lost. But because of many, like you, embodying the loving light of All That Is and expressing the wonderful possibilities as the rebirth of humanity begins to unfold, there is nothing for anyone to fear.

As you allow these changes to unfold, you will find ease if you breathe deeply, feel your heart beating, feel the loving pulse of All That Is leading you to the seat within the temple in your heart. The cascade of loving will astound you. The beings on the other planet we introduced you to know this possibility as their own great truth. We ask you to breathe with us and open to the possibilities awaiting you, welcoming them as they appear to you. This is a tool for becoming anchored within the moment, within the now, allowing the expression you bring into reality to be one of joy, fun, and play.

Be at ease as this process accelerates. You are still undergoing many changes and alterations within the frequency of humanity. There are many celestial bodies, planets, stars, suns, who are acting in concert, supporting you, allowing these processes to accelerate at this time. Many physical, non-physical, seen and unseen beings are also in co-operation with these ideals. These beings know, feel and understand that they are the loving expression of All That Is and wish to allow these energies to cradle you and lift you into the awareness of this truth.

But, as the agreements stand, all who are involved in loving and teaching you humans can only show you the possibilities. It is up to you to step into this truth with open minds and open hearts, loving and embracing yourselves. We love you and wish for you to embrace yourselves as we embrace you, so you may feel support and ease within this process.

You are the living loving breath of All That Is and this is reflected within all aspects of your Self. This is where you find your true loving nature and begin to understand the truth of who you are. We love you as we love ourselves. We share and broadcast these loving frequencies, making them available to you. Through our songs and our breath, we assist in changing the frequencies within this physical reality. We offer these frequencies, these vibrations of love, to you from the very center of our beingness, from the core of All That Is.

We are the Whales in you.

7

Shifting Frequencies

We, the Whales, are in joy to share our understanding with you. We come as the same two whales who have been with you on this journey through the inner workings of creation. The oneness we feel as Self seated within the void is ever present. Breathe with us as we create the alignment and opening for this message to infiltrate your consciousness, into your unique perspective. Open your heart to the truth of your desire to expand and connect in the loving silence, the peaceful motionless depth of the void, where we all truly exist as the oneness.

We are here as your teachers. We wish nothing more than to allow you to remember the agreements we all made in the beginning. Within you is a memory, a deep desire, embedded within your soul Self, a calling to become the **Record Keepers**, the Librarians of Truth, as we are.

All that is expressed or experienced is eternal. We, the Whales, as caretakers of the Library of Cycles, are aware of and preserve all expression, experience, interpretations, impressions, and feelings ever created, and have studied the stored holographic records and images of these memories beyond time. This library is vast and is connected within all realities, within all paradigms, through all dimensions throughout all creation. As humans expand their awareness and express their willingness to become the librarians, as we are now, the abilities will be found within you to understand and comprehend what the records of cycles truly contain. You will learn to transform your vibrational frequency so as to allow you to enter any paradigm or reality you desire. This is part of the process that allows individuals to record, absorb, remember and share information.

Within our awareness as librarians, we have access to all holograms. We can enter a hologram containing the diverse experiences, feelings, knowledge, truth and wisdom of a particular individual expression which has been recorded as they played out their lifetime. Through the process of learning to be the librarians and through the exploration of the memories stored within this library, you will see, in truth, who you are. As you gain abilities to gracefully change your vibration you can explore and expand into the frequencies embedded within the spheres of memories. Here we will discuss the idea of shifting vibrational frequency from this physical, temporal reality.

As All That Is, we are aware of all our choices. We each can choose to experiment and to explore new and diverse experiences beyond a particular reality of physical form. The truth is, your identity as soul Self, or divine awareness, is unchanged, though you are continuously changing your manifestations throughout creation. You have allowed yourself, or parts of yourself, to harmonize, resonate or tune to slower frequencies, as in this denser reality for example, where you are experiencing expression now.

When awareness of your true self as the oneness arises through all of the many expressions of form you have created, you gain the opportunity to combine, harmonize, match or expand the frequencies expressed as density. Opening to the memories of creation stored in the library allows a review or survey from which you can compare, and contrast experiences. This is the playing field!

Shifting your vibration from within your heart leads to the recalibration of your physical awareness and embodied senses. As you open to this truth you will find that the energy required to make the changes in your vibration is less than you might imagine. It is the belief in what is possible which is changing within humanity. Sing with us as we dive deep into this truth.

Breathe within your open heart. Breathe love!

* * *

We have been the librarians for many grand cycles and as you awaken to the memory of choosing to become the same, we facilitate an activation within you by sharing particular frequencies of the loving breath of All That Is. As these frequencies flow through us to you, we allow a deconstruction of the tones so that you may integrate the frequencies through the combinations of notes available to you now, to create a harmony for allowing a recalibration of your senses, of your perceptions and abilities to see and understand a fuller spectrum of reality. As you expand your awareness within this denser form, you can see, feel and know these subtler energies for what they are.

Feel deeply within the space between breaths. In this moment, within each pulse of love, is where the changes within your vibrational frequency signature can be expressed. For all is in this moment. All is one, in this now. Now is within. Now opens to the memories, the expressions, allowing them to appear before you. Now is the opening we breathe. The space between the breaths is the focal point for this Now. This is where the connection to yourself as Self occurs. As you touch and feel this point within you, the truth becomes brighter and allows your Self, as All That Is, to express and play within any reality you wish.

The timing for the collective shift is coming into alignment. The awareness of your agreement to become the librarians is just beginning to unfold within the collective consciousness of humanity.

The tools and the technology for changing frequencies will become available to you, giving you access to all the information, truth, wisdom, feelings and memories contained within the Library of Cycles. This library is vast and contains diverse experiences from many different life forms, many that are still unrecognizable to you at this point of your evolution as humans.

As your heart opens to the true understanding and experience of unconditional love, fear fades and peace within this knowing arises. As you become clearer and understand this concept within yourself, you will gain more ability to change your vibration. Through love you will be able to explore these holograms and the expressions contained within them.

Humankind has come so very far and the spark contained within your form, the core aspect of your Self, the star child you are, is where this all began. These agreements were made long before you became humans. The desire, the joy, the understanding of what you will gain in your evolution, brought great joy to you and now in this moment that joy can still be felt, touched and known as you allow yourself to embrace the oneness and the individual aspect, combined.

As you became human, as you embodied denser forms from the original star seed, a combination of frequencies allowed the shifting of matter, of energy, of light, to be contained and configured within your desires. You have always had these abilities. It is part of how we all create as the oneness, how we allow the individual expressions to become form manifest. The feeling, the knowing, the interaction of these frequencies is truly a multidimensional technology, a multidimensional art that allows the recombination of energies to create pathways to what we wish to experience.

As we, the Whales, individually and collectively, desire to move from one reality to another, we connect to the desired frequency we wish to explore. We breathe our oneness, our knowingness of our Selves as All That Is, through our hearts and into the frequency we wish to explore. It is a subtle movement of the breath, for we do not wish to overpower or disturb the frequency we are choosing to explore. As we become the new frequency, allowing it to harmonize within our breath as All That Is, we travel within the inner layers of creation. As we move from one perspective of reality to the other, it is very similar to what has been creatively envisioned by some as traveling through wormholes. But the truth is you are actually allowing a shifting of frequencies within yourselves and as the shift occurs you see the in-between space of creation. This is of a paradoxical nature because movement is only a temporal perception.

Within physical or manifest forms, we create to be able to express, to love, and find joy in experiences. The denser realities appear as motion through time. Where, as the oneness, all we do is change perspective, focus and desire. The understanding of this ability, of traveling through one dimension into another with ease, is a matter of the broader perception of the grand reality within the expression of creation. Full spectrum awareness!

Remember, as we connect as one in the loving silence of the void, we gain the ability to consciously become anything we choose. When you allow yourself to merge with this understanding, you will feel the expansion we all share as one, within every expression you become. This is how we play and find joy. All beings truly desire to express and love each other in the joy of being an individual. We are within everything that is expressed and the reflections we become to each other remind us of this truth. We create to exist, we exist to create, to become more. We become more as we choose to love our Self as All That Is. This is the truth beyond all truths.

We, the whales, are in great joy as we consciously choose to share this with all of humanity. We ask that you allow yourself the time, the space and the opening to expand even more. We are guiding you and loving you.

We are the Whales in you.

8

The Timeless Arena of Loving

We, the Whales, have created many openings for you, many expressions of our loving songs and breath, in the desire for you to find the loving songs within yourself. Breathe within your heart as we now swim together.

We are offering an opportunity for a new understanding of how the expression of life creates pathways for your ascension. Singing your joy within the knowing that all is a reflection of Self, allows this perception to be incorporated within your reality, freeing you to soar through your awareness, jumping and leaping to new heights as you open the doorway to the loving breath of All That Is.

The belief in the necessity of moving through one step or level at a time is part of your old paradigm. In the new realities you will no longer need to limit yourself with these beliefs. Accelerating your awakening, becoming your true self within the loving breath of All That Is, is the dream we all share for you. Listen to the truth within the breath. Allow your awareness to open to the possibilities of expanded realities within your heart.

As you integrate the truth we share remember the loving breath of All That Is flowing through you is key to creating your paradise. Heaven on earth is expressed through your heart, through the loving breath, as you find joy within what is in front of you now. In joy and love the opening is found, allowing heaven on earth to become your reality in the now. As humanity learns to express through the heart, the creations or manifestations that appear will be a true reflection of this loving breath.

Focus your attention in your heart and express joy, allowing it to be your truth. Sing, play and dance within your open hearts as you express this loving breath to each other, to Gaia, and to all creatures that live upon and within her. She feels joy for you. As you open to the love you are, feel her as she continuously breathes her love into your awareness. Breathing and sharing this love collectively is a way to allow the dreams you are carrying as the collective humanity to become reality here on our beautiful planet.

Breathe with us as we open an alignment to expand you even further. Feel our connection as it embraces and engulfs you, opens and loves you. Expand your awareness into the void. Breathe this expansiveness throughout your body and into the earth. Ground and center yourself as Self seated in your heart temple. Allow yourself to feel the joy in the unconditionally loving expression of the divine nature of Self. Reach out your awareness to embrace all you see before you, for these expressions are reflections of your true nature as the loving being you are. The allowing reveals joy and beauty in your physical manifestations. As you breathe the loving breath through you, as you become the loving breath, feel our connection in the void and notice the thread weaving its way through your physical reality.

Stay centered within your heart where the connection to divine reality exists, the connection to who you are as full spectrum awareness. By expressing through your divinity, expressing as the loving breath of All That Is, you can easily allow the shift in perspective within yourself to perceive heaven on earth. The idea of heaven can be translated as unconditionally loving and embracing everything that is part of your reality, allowing the perfection that is the loving breath of All That Is.

Allow yourself to feel the love, beauty and joy flowing into your core and embrace these reflections of your own divine awareness. This is the path for creating balance in your world as you see the value and perfection in all expressions reflecting back to you. You are not separate from creation. You are an integral part of all you observe, of all you participate in.

Through our teaching we express to all beings why it is essential to live within your heart and love the now as it appears to you. We love you within the now, within the knowingness as it appears within the now. The loving light we share is our Selves, as expressions reflecting the loving light of All That Is. In the now we are timeless. In the now all of creation is before us and within us. In the now we find our true empowerment as divine awareness.

In the now, within our hearts, we can transform our energetic frequency, we can travel and expand. By connecting with each other in the now we create the loving web that supports us. In this moment, as you open to these loving energies and allow them to flow through your heart, the experience and expression of love becomes who you are within all the realities you choose to express in, within all you desire, creating your heaven on Earth.

We, the Whales, live this truth with every breath we take. Being present in the moment is where we allow the expressions and the connections to find the truth of who we are. We exist in the timeless void and this is where we call you from. It is from here we send our loving songs into all that you have allowed to be created within your realities. As our breath enters you and your creations, our two realities intersect, and this brings you ever closer to us and to the understandings we wish to share with you. We have shared this within many of your lifetimes. Many humans have found this truth within themselves by hearing our call, by listening to our songs and they have been sharing this wisdom with humanity for as long as you have existed within and on this planet. It is not necessary for you to know our history but we are asking you to allow this truth of living in the now to become your guiding truth, your awareness and your expression.

We, the Whales, are waiting for your loving embrace, in the now as we breathe our love together. We are creating a synergistic connection for our true joy in working side by side, Humans and Whales, together.

Here in the stillness of this moment, stretch your awareness into the expanse, into the void, through all the creations expressed within the fabric of the universal mind. The filaments within the universal mind weave through, in between and all around the loving web of life we all are creating together. These cords of light contain the frequencies of loving we all express as they reach through all of the creations we have allowed through our breath. Our personal energetic signatures remain as unique creations in and of themselves and are imprinted within all we have experienced and learned through the expansion we are creating, in this now. As we are seated in the heart temple, in the void, we can see the energetic patterns forming around us like the colorful threads in a tapestry being woven with light.

Through many cycles we all have created what we desire, both consciously and unconsciously. The loving pulse of All That Is flows through us as we breathe and energize our expressions, our manifestations, creating new patterns, new life, new reflections.

You have created your reality from these finer, subtle energies and allowed slower, more dense expressions to manifest as your material world, as your physical body. These creations, these reflections of your Self, are always encoded with the truth of who you are. There is a direct connection between physical reality and your existence within the void, as the loving breath of All That Is. The frequency of unconditional divine love is unchanging. The vibration of the loving breath we breathe here in the void flows through all dimensional realities, through all layers of creation. By allowing yourself to embrace and become the loving breath, this current, this loving pulse flowing through everything, connects you to your true Self as All That Is.

Within the loving breath, as divine beings, we express love to you and through you. As you allow this love to penetrate deep within your awareness, you begin to awaken to your own divinity. We ask you to anchor your divinity into the reality your body exists in, in the now, allowing it to flow into the earth and into all the creations you express, or witness through your mind, through your hands, through every embrace you give and receive. This alignment is in the now. The loving breath flowing through everything is in the moment we share. We live always in this moment. This practice accelerates your awakening to your true Self within.

Linear time, as you feel it within your mind, within your third dimensional reality, is a mechanism that allows your physical creations to come to life through your interactions and collaborations. Your perception of time allows you to see and process the birth and expression of atoms and molecules becoming form. This is the process of expressing your true loving nature within all manifestation you bring forth as divine creators. The loving breath of All That Is permeates all life, all forms. Atoms and molecules come together within their own awareness and perspective, agreeing to be the creations you bring into existence. They agree to serve. They agree to collaborate with us. They agree to love, just as we do. We are all this loving breath of creation. All desire to be here in the now as the loving breath of All That Is.

Let us embrace you in this moment as we share the Dream of All That Is. Settle gently into your Self, open to the memories that have been stored through all eternity, throughout all creation. This is all available to you. You need only ask. All divine beings, your Angels, Guides, Ascended Masters, are your loving friends and are allowing the loving breath to flow through them to be felt by you. They are willing to help you, to serve your ascension. But without you asking, all they can do is watch, ready for your call. They have gone through much of what you are experiencing now. By asking them and allowing their help, they will be willing to share all of their truth, all of their wisdom, just as we, the Whales, do.

We sing to you and as you allow our songs to enter you, we find joy in the sharing, in the loving, creating a circle that completes and connects us, remembering that we are one within our hearts. This is our truth expressed. As we send our awareness out through the filaments of the loving web of creation and encounter another being, we find our Self reflected back to us as we gaze into each other's eyes. We are supporting and loving ourselves as we express our individuality from within our hearts. For without our Selves as reflections, the **songs of living** would not be so diverse, so intricate, so vibrant. This is why we play and dance, this is why we sing and create. We are infinitely beautiful as this one breath.

We love you and allow the loving breath we are to flow through everything we touch. As you see your Self expressed within your individuality, that awareness branches throughout all creation. This is the loving web, the universal mind, creating connections within the physical mind and body. All of these are reflections of the living loving breath of All That Is.

And as you open your brain's synapses to the universal mind, activating them through your Self as you are seated within your heart temple, you will begin to gain the knowledge of how to change frequencies, of how to travel within your perceptual reality. It is a subtle shifting within your perspective that allows you to consciously become, expand and create beyond what you have known up until now. In the process of creating or manifesting, you pull your reality out of and express through the fabric of space, the fabric of the universal mind. It is an emerging, it is a becoming, it is an allowing. These are the true expressions of creation as the oneness we are.

As you allow and open to these ideas and images, we are filled with great joy and ecstasy. We love you.

We are the Whales in you.

9

Light Expanding
Within Your Heart

Breathe deeply. Dive in and connect with us, the same two sperm whales who have been swimming with you on this part of your journey. See us waiting for you in the sacred circle. As you float nearer, notice a flash of light erupting between us, illuminating our blue gray forms. Look into our soft eyes expressing our loving feelings to you. Do not be afraid as we draw you closer.

We open a connection with you to bring the light of truth to your awareness, to your heart, to your mind. Allow the connection that the two elements, of our breath as Self and the pulse of All That Is, create within you. It is these elements we, the Whales, employ to learn and grow, to know and become the two beings you see sitting before you. The illuminating spark between us is the light from within your heart expanding, allowing you to see with your mind's eye.

We, the Whales, are within your heart, within your mind, within your body, within the structure of your beingness. We breathe our loving breath into you as you open your heart, filling every part of you with the love we are, the love of All That Is.

Feeling this illuminating force within your heart, allowing it to expand into your awareness, creates a way for you to see and understand the many realities within all of our creations. As humanity opens to the possibilities within themselves this spark illuminates the Self, allowing you to see your full potential.

Listen deeply within your open heart. Allow the loving breath of All That Is to flow within you, propelling you on your exploration within the expanse, within your heart, within all creations throughout existence. Bring your desire into focus. Ask your questions. Voice your requests. As your thoughts flow out into the expanse, into the universal mind, carried on the loving breath of All That Is, they will connect with the precise images and holograms stored within the vast mind of all of creation. Within and instant, faster than light, faster than thought, faster than the imagination, the answer to your question is within your mind's eye, within your heart.

This information can expand your understanding, give deeper meaning to your experience and help you explore more possibilities within the multidimensional realities. This is available to lend ease and grace on your journey through expanding existence and offers you great resources for creating your heart's desire. As humanity's awareness expands, the ability to manifest physical form, or create realities by pulling directly from the fabric of the universe, will become more conscious, more obvious.

Breathe deeply as you open your heart and begin to see and feel these images within your mind. As you come into coherence with the finer frequencies of creation, you will find the ability to venture into diverse realities. As your body resonates within these new frequencies and you sing or broadcast them back into your reality, the awakening within your current physical form accelerates. You will feel it! You literally feel and sing your way into alternate realities.

Feel deep within. Listen between breaths. Observe through the cycling of your own heartbeat and the cycling of your thought patterns. Imagine yourself in the place beyond the cycles, between the layers that have appeared as form, to where Self is seated in the void. This is where we all exist as awareness. We are all observers and listeners within the stillness. Connect with your Self in this depth, beyond all words, beyond all thoughts, beyond all creation that has been expressed. Deep within your core, look for the truth of who you are and who we are. We are the formless. We are eternal. We are the spark of light illuminating the dreams we share, the songs we sing as we know our Selves reflecting love back to our Selves in a harmonic dance of creation. Here is the beginning of all things, the beginning of all expression.

As we each create a new frequency or harmonic within the breath, it is broadcast out in all directions.

Like the image of a pebble dropped into water, sending out little waves across a pond, bouncing little leaves and water bugs on the surface, running into the shore and bouncing off other objects in the pond. The pebble that creates the waves is our breath, our desire, our intent, our consciousness expanding into the void. Our breath, our song, interacts with everything it touches and is reflected back to us. As those waves or frequencies encounter other surfaces, other spheres of creation, other boundaries, an impression is reflected back, creating another wave or frequency. This frequency is altered by the qualities of what it has touched, if even only subtly, and finds its way back to us, informing us, enriching us, expanding into us. As the waves or frequencies intersect, a web is woven and together we create the fabric of the universe.

In the center of our awareness, in the void as Self, as infinite potential, we express our unique frequency, our unique energetic signature. With our own breath and with the loving pulse of All That Is, we sing to move energy. These two elements, our breath as Self and the pulse of All That Is, create light. This illumination happens on the edge of our awareness, on our periphery. As this light illuminates our surrounding creations, we see, feel, hear, experience and exist. All around you are other individual divine sparks singing and allowing illumination to occur.

We, the Whales, have touched this depth within our Selves and even deeper. By opening your hearts and breathing our love, inhaling our love, you are allowing your focus to open to your Self seated within illumination, broadcasting, receiving and connecting to all other individual spheres of creation expressing in this manner.

Depending on your point of view, we can appear to be closer or further apart. This is just a choice of perspective, for we are all one. As you remember this truth within yourself, you can feel the connections that exist within the emptiness. As you expand yourselves and open to even more, you find your Selves within the depths and know your Selves as the infinite awareness of All That Is.

Breathe deeply. Follow the lighted pathway, the golden cord, back to your body and open your vision to see us sitting here in circle with you. We have chosen the expressions we are sharing within our visions of ourselves. This is the reality where we allow our creations to expand, the 'in between' of the layers of the web, where we create together. Atoms and molecules come together to shape the expressions we pull from the matrix, from the clay of the void, from the connections and the multi-dimensional frequencies of this playing field of love. The expressions take form and awaken to their own awareness, their own hearts. Just as the birthing of our physical children is allowing life to continue, the birthing of our energetic creations allows the process of conscious evolution to expand as these creations take on an existence and consciousness of their own.

Within the **cycles of impermanence**, within the reality of the body, each unique being, each expression has the opportunity to expand in aware-ness. As our light grows, as our understanding and knowing become expanded, we have the ability to fully and consciously experience the flow and rhythm of our unique frequency as we explore and create. All this expansion is occurring simultane-ously as we breathe our truth and express our Selves from within the loving breath of All That Is. By allowing yourself to become the breath seated within the center of your awareness, you can see all of creation vibrating, singing, breathing, becoming and feel the divine loving pulse flowing through the frequencies within every expression, within the beauty we witness as the shared joy we are creating.

In the silence of the void we can detect the slightest motion, hear the slightest sound. Even light has tone, like music. What appears within our awareness as form are the tones we have broadcast from within our core, from the center of our Selves. Frequency, vibration and harmonics are what we use to create. This is what we refer to when we say we are singing and breathing our reality into being. What you hear with your physical ears and see with your physical eyes is only a tiny fraction of the infinite spectrum of frequency available throughout creation.

As your human mind touches this truth and understands expressing the loving breath within the heart, allowing the frequencies to expand, broadcast and echo between us as we have described, you are witnessing the process of our 'Self' loving all we are and all we have become. This is our play, our purpose, our truth. From the very first breath, the web or template of creating was set in motion. This is the infinite expansion of the loving breath of All That Is.

As you begin to experience the direct connection you are as Self to All That Is, this information, this energy, these frequencies can transform your awareness to fully experience reality in its interdimensionality as the divine being you are. Allow yourself to be guided by the loving breath of All That Is.

We, the Whales, use these tools, this information, this knowingness and now we are teaching this to you. Do not hold onto these words as the truth, but as reflections of the truth. They are just vehicles to allow you to step deeper into your own heart, into the oneness.

We love you. We are in joy you are finding the infinite truth within your paradigm, in the reality we are expressing together here on earth. This is the transition into eternity, into infinite awareness. As you begin to understand and feel this you will never lose your way again.

We know in truth who you are. You are the divine spark of light radiating from within the void, illuminating all you create.

We are the Whales in you.

10

Stepping Into Oneness

We, the two whales who have been communicating with you throughout these meditations, are offering you concepts and tools to help you open to a broader awareness of your current paradigm. See us as we float in through your heart, swirling in a vortex of energy, swimming in vertical loops, surrounded in beautiful multicolored pulsing light, singing our joy as we connect and become one breath.

Our awareness stretches far beyond the realities within your vision. You may wonder if we have names and yes we do, but the truth we share is beyond the idea of having names. As we breathe and expand our awareness of Self, embracing all embodiments we have experienced, the names are countless. In truth we identify our singularity by our unique energetic signature, the pattern of light we are creating, that we are expressing throughout our existence. We are not just one name, one color, one thread, one tone, one note. We are each an unending symphony broadcasting our unique melody throughout creation, just as you are also doing.

We embrace you within this awareness, within your heart, within all we are and all you are. Allow yourself to relax into the oneness. Breathe deeply into your heart and allow it to expand as we bring our frequencies into alignment.

We, the Whales, experience many diverse realities. We are witnessing new ideas emerging from within the human collective consciousness. The way you perceive and create is changing. We are bringing the Library of Cycles, and all the holograms of memories stored therein, to your awareness. Through awakening to and embracing your full spectrum Self, you can allow your perception, your awareness, to interact with the Library of Cycles.

This library stores holograms or spheres, encapsulating the memories, thoughts, feelings and experiences expressed within the reality of an individual being creating the frequencies. These are the expressions and impressions created within the lifespan of an individual being as they moved through their life processes. They are imprinted within the universal mind and stored within the vast Library of Cycles.

These holographic memories are reflections of your Self as All That Is. They are a resource to help you navigate and consider your experience as you wonder how to proceed and choose what to express or manifest. The important aspect of gazing into these holographic patterns is the feelings and visions that present themselves as you are seated within your heart temple.

These memories may appear as an overview, an essence, a fragrance, a flavor or sensation from a broader perspective but still contain the total recorded experience, just not focusing on the linear details but on the overall impression of the total experience. One can follow the memory directly back to the actual experience and choose to relive it if desired. There are no boundaries, no restrictions. From the perspective of the oneness we see the full range of experience, without judgment and rejoice in the ecstasy of this expansive process, far beyond any concept of joy or ecstasy that you as temporal humans as yet can fathom. As embodied beings you are focusing on a very narrow range of frequencies and are deeply exploring, learning, and integrating these particular frequencies at this moment. And the universe rejoices in your experiences.

Because of the impermanent, continuously flowing nature of cycles, memories are held within the timelessness of the void, within eternity, to always be available for access by the individual perspective, and by the collective as well. These spheres of memories, these holograms, can be accessed through the universal mind, through the fabric of space, beyond time, beyond all creations. The wisdom stored within becomes part of you as you open your heart and gaze into, or resonate with them, feeling the breath contained within them. A knowing will arise within you. As you perceive from within your heart, the diverse multi-dimensional frequencies contained therein will be understood. For we, as All That Is, appreciate beyond the singularity what these memories in the Library of Cycles contain.

Breathe with us and find your Self within your heart, expressing the joy that is the opening, the allowing, and the discovering within your awareness. As your perceptions pierce the veil, as your awareness expands, you will be able to grasp, to comprehend, the multidimensional diversity of all creation, and translate that information into the particular space where you are now seated.

We, the Whales, as Self, reside within our hearts. We focus and allow different frequencies to express within our unconditional perception. We find joy within all expressions, within all frequencies, for they are all part of the loving breath, the living breath of All That Is. Within this knowingness, all is seen as reflections of love.

We, the Whales, are excited you are engaging in the process of allowing your focus to shift and embracing your alternate realities in a coherent perspective within the singularity you are. This is creating much joy within many paradigms of reality.

We, the Whales, see how this is opening and expanding humanity, within the loving light, within the loving pulse we are sharing with you. The choices along the path of your growing awareness are just that, yours. We choose to be within our creations, expressing our loving gratitude, our joy, our connections, and breathing as one within all of our hearts, together. Your unique way of expressing allows you to unfold your Self, for yourself.

As you feel the flow and come into resonance with the loving breath of All That Is, we know the expressions you allow to become form will bring great joy to all of us. As joy fills your heart, it is broadcast through the loving web of creation into all of our hearts. This is but one understanding of the depth of ecstasy and joy we feel as we sing within the void that connects us all together, within the loving web. It is a profound feeling, beyond what your mind and body have yet understood. But your body and mind are changing and will soon touch this reality. You will come to know it is safe to allow yourself to become seated within your core as Self, allowing these connections within the loving web to be felt and expressed.

Can you feel the loving embrace as we all experience and sing our joy for the creations we each have expressed within our own perspective? Ecstasy and joy flow through the filaments of the web of life, combining with more joy in each loving breath. These frequencies of love are amplified and arise from within our Self as an ecstatic encounter beyond expression itself. Through this experience we embrace ourselves as the loving breath of All That Is, becoming more deeply immersed within the expression of joy, knowing as this arises from within our Self, the sharing of these frequencies engages the oneness that is our connection within all hearts throughout existence. Everything is connected!

Allow yourself to feel the peaceful loving ecstasy and joy throughout your entire being as you become centered in the truth that we are the loving breath as All That Is. Feel the joy. Feel the ecstasy. Breathe it into your physical reality. Breathe it into your body. Let it expand your connection to the oneness we share within our hearts. As joy builds and flows through you, joy is reflected back to All That Is through the singularity you are, allowing us all to expand and know the profound beauty within the creations we each become. This energy, this love, flows in both directions at once through the connection to All That Is. As we allow the divine flow, we are all this, loving as All That Is. As you become more aware of this flow within your everyday experience of the moment, the connections become stronger, more profound, and you will touch the experience of knowing we are all infinite and eternal.

Perceiving from within the heart space will always lead you to the truth, to the love expressed by us all within the oneness as the loving breath of All That Is. As you fully embrace these memories, the web we are cradled by is activated and energized, allowing unending expression within the *flower of life*. You are awakening to the processes of how you create vessels to experience and express through. As these vessels shift, change frequencies, are reclaimed, becoming part of the process once more, you will never lose sight of the essence, the spark, the unique expression you are.

We, the Whales, practice and are teaching you the *way of allowing*. We feel, remember and connect, using purity of breath and intention to create our experience, allowing the loving breath that flows from the oneness to be expressed through us, into all of us.

Through the remembering and allowing, we have learned to travel far and wide within many dimensional realities and manifestations, in and out of time. Within the expression of oneness, within the expression of singularity, within the awareness of the realities we have created, we flow continuously, feeling joy and ecstasy within the void, within our hearts. The connection lives within the loving embrace of who we are as the love of All That Is. We expand together in this wisdom of connection and infuse our awareness with a feeling of completeness and wholeness.

The loving joy you express is like a switch, or a valve allowing these energies to flow, moving in an infinite helical pattern, a cycling pattern. As the ecstatic feelings arise from within your heart, and our frequencies connect and engage, you allow loving pulses to flow through all of us, all of creation. As you embrace and are saturated by your own love and joy, the light emerging from your core intensifies and echoes ecstasy into your surroundings, into the creations of life you perceive and into the reflections, the memories, the knowingness in all we have created together as the loving light of All That Is.

Divine light fills all realities, all creations, reflecting the truth back to you, generating yet another cycle, another wave, infusing more joy and ecstasy into all dimensional realities we are, have been and will express. Joy activates these circuits of energy. As you embrace the joy, the dancing, the playing within your loving breath, you are communicating your true desire for experiencing more loving joy to the universal mind and it will be reflected back to you and into your world.

*   *   *

If you allow your mind to continue to create form from the limiting belief of judgment and duality, [i.e.: the struggle between negative/positive, good/evil, fear/love, flow/stagnation, etc.] the universal mind will show you just that, reinforcing your belief in conflict. When you clearly understand the limiting nature of the perceptions and beliefs previously held within your third dimensional world mindset and release them, you then have a greater opportunity to incorporate and play in the finer, faster frequencies. The limiting beliefs your mind perceives as truth, or real, will become obsolete.

As you shift your awareness to your heart temple and create from the oneness as the loving breath, from the vantage point of a broader perspective of loving, the reality or life you create will be a clearer reflection of balance, of your full spectrum Self with the awareness you are as love. By simply shifting your focus you will become more adept in your expression of your bodies, your vessels, as conduits of light. When you consciously express as the oneness within the finer dimensional frequencies, collectively creating a balanced, harmonious shared experience as humanity, the ecstasy will be felt throughout the loving web of creation and the quickly manifesting expressions will reveal your true alignment with who you are as love.

As you incorporate your understanding of the finer frequencies, your perceptions of the third dimensional reality will change. As you open your heart, new codes or frequencies of light interact with your DNA structure and shift the physical vessels you are seated in. When you anchor the finer energetic frequencies into your body, you will be physically able to conduct and maintain more light, more of the loving breath of All That Is, through you and project the ecstatic joyous feeling of being held in a loving embrace back into the paradigm you create personally & collectively. This will manifest heaven on earth in your day to day experience. This is where you begin to consciously and coherently express within the fifth dimensional realities and above.

We, the Whales, are observing you shift your perspective and come into resonance with these finer frequencies. We see the expression of your new paradigm actually becoming what you experience. The keys allowing you to change and increase your vibrational resonance with the subtler, finer dimensional realities, are held within your heart. They are the joy and peace in the knowingness we are all one within the breath of All That Is. Within the finer dimensional realities, where we all express, play and sing our joy, we are brought ever closer in the connection to the oneness of All That Is. The growing awareness, the becoming, the knowing of this truth within your heart, allows the loving breath of All That Is to expand further.

We, the Whales, have only begun to understand this truth. For the depth of this truth cannot be held even within our awareness. But we know and feel this embrace through the deepest part of our Self, feeling the connection, the oneness we are as All That Is. We maintain this truth as we express and create. This is our conduit to fathomless joy! We, as All That Is, have chosen to be ever expanding, ever experiencing, ever sharing, ever breathing, ever becoming and living the expressions of existence from within our Selves.

Within your thinking process there will always be a paradoxical nature to this truth. Can you see and hear the expressions of the thinking mind and understand it is part of the process of creating? When you breathe your loving breath into these thoughts, acknowledging their existence, finding joy from within whatever pattern they create, you can embrace them and know them for the truth they are. This is where the opportunity for changing your thoughts finds a profound application. Remember, your thoughts are the blueprint for creating your reality.

By touching the depths of your Self as the loving breath of All That Is and completing the circuit of love and joy within your physical awareness, within your mind, within all of your third dimensional reality, you create a pathway for your true divinity to flow into your world. As you fully express in a consciously connected, coherent way, you create in alignment with the unlimited joy and ecstasy available from within the oneness we are as All That Is.

As you become clearer within the creating process and clearer about the true representations of what you desire, you will be able to refocus your awareness into different realities, to observe many expressions of love and see your Self therein. Within the core of your Self as the loving breath of All That Is, the ability to flow into all the expressions that are you will become easier and you will experience clarity about how this is accomplished, or allowed. Soon it will become a normal pattern within your awareness. This is just a heartbeat, just a breath away. The shifting of your perception is within reach and as you practice what we have shared, you will recognize the openings and have confidence to easily step through the illusions.

We, the Whales, are holding and embracing you and all humans with the loving truth of our Self, teaching and sharing all we have learned through all our existence, through all our investigation into the depths, all the experiences we have expressed, leading us deeper into the truth of the reality of our infinite nature. Allow the gentleness of our embrace to nurture you into becoming aware of who you truly are within your Self.

We find great joy in sharing our love for you and in sharing these processes within your mind, within our mind, within your heart, within our heart. We love you. We embrace you with the loving light of All That Is, the pure light of Source, as it flows through, back, around and into all we are, allowing us to go deeper into the oneness, into the memories and connections as All That Is and back again to our singular awareness. We ride on these waves, these loving breaths into any reality, paradigm or dimension we choose. The deeper we go into the memory of our truth as love, the more we become love, pure awareness, growing brighter, exploring beyond imagination.

We are the Whales in you.

11

Conscious Living
Within the Finer Frequencies

We, the Whales, greet you with love and the deepest respect for what you, as humans, are undertaking. As we swim into your awareness, we are joined by a third sperm whale, a great master who understands the primal aspect of creation through geometry, which is present in the matrix of this paradigm.

We three whales are swimming fin-to-fin, swirling in a vortex together, creating a pathway, a connection, a triad, joining and weaving many physical and non-physical energy fields together. The connection and blending of our three frequencies creates a harmonic expansion beyond what your dualistic reality has, up until now, allowed. The dimensions we are conveying are of a magnitude beyond your current paradigm. We are making many new dimensional frequencies available to your physical reality.

As we express in this way, breathing together as one from three, expansion is allowed for the activation of movement. Through our connection, we see the expression of our desire accelerated. The field of energy the synchronized breath creates, allows growth and learning beyond what your current physical reality has revealed and supported. The pathway to a clearer understanding of these inter-dimensional realities is through a triad, through the connection of three.

By expressing love within yourself and together, as you collectively harmonize the desire within your hearts and synchronize your expression into a single tone, movement is felt, and an expression is brought into reality. The expression of this truth is reflected in all you witness. It is part of the matrix we all share. It is what we all do, together.

Through understanding the frequencies of existence, everything can be changed, allowing an opening, an awareness, a freedom beyond all limitations, even allowing you to move between dimensional realities. Once this idea is set into motion in your minds, you will expand into a clearer understanding. The alignment that allows us, the Whales, to travel within different dimensional realities will begin to be expressed and known within human consciousness. This is not of a nature of being focused with the mind but of allowing the natural order of the expression within the matrix to occur. As you expand your awareness, joined with the understanding of the subtle nature of energy, you can utilize these frequencies.

We, the two sperm whales who have authored these messages, have invited a great mathematician to join our circle. This whale is an interdimensional traveler who has the understanding of the geometric nature of creation, the nature of the templates that create the physical and celestial bodies, that create the universe, and the many paradigms associated with maintaining this universe. This whale embraces both the divine masculine and the divine feminine as it is part of the template of creation. Without these aspects the essence of the balancing nature of energy would not be revealed.

113

He has the ability to travel through all aware-
nesses, dimensions and realities. His purpose is to
help maintain and allow the cycling of creations
through this geometric understanding. He offers his
assistance in balancing the energies involved with
the natural patterns of life. He does not adjust or
move the patterns but he helps allow the energy
that may become restricted to realign and flow
once again. He does not create these geometric
patterns, he just understands them on the deepest
level. These patterns are the templates created in
the beginning and are in motion continuously. Just
as your human body is in its own process of living
and expresses its form as itself, these templates are
of a similar nature. They have their own awareness,
their own intelligence, their own processes that by
their very nature provide us with opportunities to
grow, experience and evolve.

Our friend wishes to speak in his own voice...

*I call you to allow me to enter your heart, for I
have much to share with you. The energies present
within my energetic signature will help you open even
deeper to the understanding of existence. I am name-
less. I am existing in many places simultaneously.*

The openings I create are beyond the linear thinking of your mind. We here within the matrix, and there are many who help facilitate these openings, many are whales, and we are spread across the galaxy, the universe and throughout the entire Grand Cycle we initiated together. We find great joy in these experiences as All That Is.

I assist the universal mind in its process of creation. I am a great master of understanding the frequencies of creation, the movement of these frequencies between diverse realities into paradigms which are calling for new frequencies and patterns, for the evolution of that particular reality. As you seek, as we all seek the evolutionary process in our awakening, so to, do these realities and paradigms which have been created for us to exist, play and express in, also desire to evolve and expand. The paradigms, the templates, are alive, are conscious and breathing with us, moving changing and expressing, together.

I have studied these structures and dedicated my existence to their understanding. I came to share with you how I am allowing, how I bringing through frequencies from diverse realities, helping to activate the awakening of your paradigm.

The swirling pattern we created as we swam into your awareness helps to stabilize this paradigm, so these new frequencies of expansion can enter your reality. Through this spinning vortex we have opened many channels that were not present up until this moment in your evolution.

My energy is associated with Sirius, the bright red star you see in your heavens. This is where I was trained, where I was initiated, the place I called home for countless millenniums. Now I call many places home. I expand, I contract, I travel, I observe, I learn. I find great joy in all of these processes. They help me evolve beyond what most whales are experiencing in this moment. It is not a judgement, it is that I have allowed myself to evolve along a path that few undertake. I feel I am of great service to all of creation. I feel evolution as it begins to ignite within, to enliven with, the spirit of All That Is.

This is the calling I felt as a young soul. My unique perspective has allowed the evolution of trillions and trillions of souls, beyond numbering. Not only living embodiments such as you, but that of many new stars and suns that are beginning to awaken within this paradigm. Through my understanding I help remind all beings that expressing within the realities they are choosing, the template and the sequencing are already established and all they need to do is breathe and be who they are, through their choices, as we all do. The template is prearranged so that we can experience ourselves on the grandest level of understanding. This supports each of us, all of us, as we evolve, awaken to and touch the infinite that we each are.

I work hand in hand with the sentient expansive template, or being, who helps maintain all of creation. We are closely associated. We communicate constantly. He is the overseer of all of this and through my service, I help maintain the adjustments he requires in order to maintain this creation for all of you.

The awakening of humans has been planned from the beginning. You humans were allowed to become who you are. You were invited as souls, as awareness, to participate in this. But there were many stagnations within the evolution of all the souls who are this grand expression, and through your awakening, your activations, through the abilities you hold, you are helping to spark this evolution once again.

The time is close for this shift, this grand opening, this surge of expansion, and within the knowing of those in the finer realities, it has already occurred.

But there are still many adjustments to be integrated, many pathways before you to be opened and journeyed upon, in order for this cycle to come to full realization.

We cannot share what exactly this change is, as yet, because telling you would not allow it to blossom in the way required for it to be fully embodied by you humans. But be at ease. Be in the love of yourself. For you are All that Is, embodied.

The ego, the games, the in and out of these playing fields you are journeying through, has all been part of the plan. Many cycles of your descent and awakening were necessary for this to unfold as it has. The 'genetic alterations' that occurred through the manipulations by the many beings who thought they were controlling you for their selfish intent, was a disguise. For the unique spark that is you, imbedded within each embodiment, could never be taken away or truly altered. Your core beingness as humans is amazingly beautiful. We are honored the we, the Whales, have been allowed to nurture you along your path of evolution into the beautiful beings we see before us. We love you.

Breathe your Self into your heart and trust that the many questions you have will be answered as you walk your path.

Balance, Collective Action, and Living This Truth as Second Nature

The pathway we three whales created the day this message was brought through will forever be present within the physical paradigm you exist in. We have expanded this reality for you to explore yourself on an even deeper level. For the depth of your Self is infinite as All That Is.

You will find balance as you become aware of the natural frequencies that arise from all of our creations within the matrix. Sing together, allowing new notes and truth to be remembered as you awaken to your Self. This is the natural state of existence. As you open to the truth of who you are as the living loving breath of All That Is, the understanding will become part of you.

We embrace you within our loving breath. Breathe and allow these concepts to be remembered in an easy and natural way. Let us help you integrate and feel this truth within your heart, within your body. View your reality from within your heart. Allow yourself to see the finer frequencies of the world around you. Allow yourself to see others around you from within your heart. Allow this to be your natural way of perceiving. Let it be second nature. See the pure loving energy that is unchanging though all dimensional realities and know the expressions are limitless.

We, the Whales, are loving you, sharing truth and wisdom with you, intertwining our breaths as one and together creating an opening for all of humanity to expand through and move into conscious life within the finer frequencies. Together our new song will echo joy throughout the universe.

We are the Whales in you, and you are the human within us.

Epilogue

All of creation celebrates your existence. The anchoring, the connections, the expansions you are bringing forth are vital to the next evolutionary step of all creation. You are invited to participate in this celebration.

Humans are embarking on a new journey. The sails of your vessel are about to fill with the breath of your true desire. Many are already shifting their dimensional awareness. Your reality has been created through many cycles and is facilitating an awakening to the expansiveness within the human heart. You each are the universe reflected back to yourselves, existing within the joy of being the unique individual you each choose to be.

The Whales have been witnessing, nurturing, allowing and supporting you to become what you have chosen. You have traversed the many experiences essential for your growth and expansion, for your awakening, and now are on the cusp of awareness to fully blossoming as divine beings of this beautiful planet, Earth.

Do not be in fear as the changes within humanity begin to occur. All who are in existence seek this change. Old beliefs are beginning to fade rapidly as many are seeking the connection of the heart. As you join each other in these choices, the synchronistic nature of changing will expand and create more possibilities for balance within your hearts and awareness.

Finding your way is simple, just breathe your living loving breath through your own heart, circulating your divinity out into the world around you, and allow it to flow back in. Harmonize your breath with the songs of your heart and let it fill all of the realities within your awareness and beyond.

Love flows through the breath. Love flows to you and through you from the finer dimensional realities, continuously. The energy of love is unchanging through all of creation. Sing this truth within your mind. Breathe this truth into your existence, remembering you are the loving breath of All That Is.

Glossary

All That Is: Source, God, Omnipotent Beingness, Spirit, Divinity

Breath Keepers: The Whales are the Breath Keepers of our planet. (And most likely, many more worlds.) With their physical conscious breathing they create balance in our world and recycle the life force in the atmosphere of Gaia. The breath is a metaphor for the Grand Cycle of Loving.

Chakras: energy centers in the body, and elsewhere

Coherent Connection: an aligned, aesthetically ordered, integrated connection. A consistent, harmonious frequency or vibration, having clarity or intelligibility; understandable. As we open and allow and become the loving light of

Source, we help bring about a greater coherent connection with all life around us and all life in the grand cycle of All That Is.

Collective Consciousness of the Whales: An assembly of masters, representing the many species of whales that have existed throughout Gaia's history, as well as the many embodiments whales have experienced in other solar systems and dimensions. They have partnered with us, the humans, from the first breath of this creation. The *Whale Collective.*

Crystal City of Ever Expanding Love, the City of Light and Hope: [see Breath of the Whales Vol. I, ch. 7.] The Whales took Keith to a temple of crystalline light, on the bottom of the ocean, in the 9th dimension. The crystalline light structures anchored there are living beings. They transform energy into frequencies that resonate throughout the 3rd, 4th, and 5th dimensional realities, operating through the grid, the web of our existence, carrying Love from Source. It is a place of great learning, a hub for many other temples around the earth and beyond.

Cycles: Grand Cycle of Learning: The many phases and manifestations of expressions of All That Is. We progress through cycles of agreements, of creating together with the many beings that we are. Each cycle is unique and has different agreements and parameters of our choosing. It is the continuous, infinite, game of life on the grandest scale. It is the way of All That is. Includes: *Galactic Cycles, Cycles of Darkness, Cycles of Impermanence.*

Flower of Life: *See Breath of the Whales Vol. I, pg. XV*

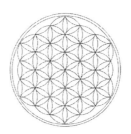

Gaia: the Earth

Ley lines: Lines or pathways of energy flowing in, through and around the earth and beyond. They are energetic arteries or highways moving energy from one location to another and hold specific patterns of creation. These lines of energy are utilized by many species for navigation.

Librarians of Truth, Memory Keepers, Record Keepers: those who collect, preserve and maintain the true history of humankind.

Library of Cycles: The record of all the patterns, impressions, vibrations, nodes, manifestations, etc. in Creation. The *Library of Knowingness.* Also referred to as the Akashic Records.

Living, Loving Breath: refers to Source energy. The unchanging energy of love from the pure potential of Creation. [or the Creator] The primal energy of existence. The Breath that animates all life. The Breath as pure awareness. The essence of All That Is in motion. [The term **Breath** is used as a metaphor for the cycling of life force, living force, light, the pure loving light of Source, Living Breath, etc.]

New Energetic Frequencies: Waves of energy from celestial bodies around us, and from distant galaxies, flow to our planet and facilitate change in the energetic patterns that exist on earth, Gaia, and all her inhabitants. [*New frequencies, new energies*]

Sacred Heart Temple: The center of our beingness, our singularity, and also the gateway to all our multidimensional realities.

Self: our singularity as pure awareness, Soul-self, divine self, higher dimensional self, etc.

Whale **Songs:** The energetic communications from whale consciousness, both singular and collective, as well as actual physical vocalizations of individual whales.

Songs of living: The interactions and combinations of frequencies we [all life] express together. Our collective symphony. The symbiotic relationship of all creation.

Truth of Creation: Love. Love is the engine of creation, of manifesting.

Universal Mind: Universal awareness, universal consciousness. The container for the awareness of All That Is, for the knowingness of All That Is. An expression of All That Is. The intelligence behind all manifested reality.

The **Void:** The infinite ocean of love and potential. Infinite potential beyond the expressed. I.e.: the unexpressed, the unmanifested.

*The **Way of Allowing:*** The opening of your heart while acknowledging and letting the flow of All That Is stream unimpeded into your reality.

About the Authors

Keith Grey Hale is the president and co-founder of Gray Whale Wisdom, Inc. He has served as a naturalist with the Santa Barbara Channel Island National Marine Sanctuary as well as served as a docent and educator at the Santa Barbara Natural History Museum Ty Warner Sea Center. Through his process of becoming a telepathic conduit for the collective consciousness of the Whales, Keith has developed a sensitivity to, and an ability to use, subtle energies and works with clients to facilitate the clearing of energetic blocks in the physical and etheric bodies, reestablishing the coherent flow of vitalizing energy, as well as energetic space clearing. Keith is also an accomplished jewelry artist and teaches silversmithing at the local adult education center.

Carolyn M Gorman is co-founder and executive director of Gray Whale Wisdom, Inc. She brings her passion for writing poetry and creative prose to the process of writing and editing inspirational works of literature. Spirit has been speaking to and through her since childhood and been a driving force in her personal and vocational journey through life.

Through cetacean science based classes and presentations, Keith and Carolyn endeavor to raise awareness about cetaceans and the human impact on our shared environment. With a focus on cetacean intelligence and communication they open a dialogue exploring a deeper perspective of consciousness and the synergistic relationship between humans and whales.

Proceeds from the sale of this book support

Gray Whale Wisdom, Inc., a nonprofit organization focused on Cetacean Education, developing enriching programs and materials to share the beauty, grace and intelligence of Whales and Dolphins. Through exploration of the broader concepts of consciousness, in regards to Cetaceans in particular, we gain a deeper understanding of the world in which we all live. The more aware and educated we are about the beings with whom we share our planet, the better prepared we will be to make conscious choices every day in all aspects of our lives. Through education and inspiration Gray Whale Wisdom strives to promote a greater appreciation for the interconnection of all life and a sense of stewardship toward our planet Earth. We have much to learn from these denizens of the sea and they are anxious to teach us!

www.GrayWhaleWisdom.org

Notes

Notes

Notes

Notes

Notes

www.BreathoftheWhales.com

Made in the USA
Charleston, SC
19 February 2017